AUTHENTIC SOUTHWESTERN COOKING

Lynn Nusom

Western National Parks Association

Tucson, Arizona

ACKNOWLEDGMENTS

Thanks to my wife, Guylyn Nusom, for her assistance in developing the recipes for this book. And thanks to my editor, Derek Gallagher, for all his help and encouragement.

About the Author: Lynn Nusom has written numerous magazine and newspaper articles and seven books on southwestern cooking including Cooking in the Land of Enchantment, The New Mexico Cook Book, The Sizzling Southwest Cookbook, Christmas in New Mexico, The Tequila Cook Book, The Billy-the-Kid Cook Book, *and* Christmas in Arizona. *He has lived in New Mexico for the past twenty-five years and he and his wife make their home in a hundred-year-old adobe, with two kitchens, in the southern part of the state.*

Library of Congress Cataloging-in-Publication Data

Nusom, Lynn.
    Authentic Southwestern Cooking/Lynn Nusom.
        p.   cm.
     ISBN 1-877856-89-4
     1. Cookery, American—Southwestern style.   I. Title.
    TX715.2.S69N85   1999
     641.5979—dc21   *98-52130*
                                                                        CIP

Published by Western National Parks Association
The net proceeds from WNPA publications support educational and research programs in the national parks.
Receive a free Western National Parks Association catalog, featuring hundreds of publications. Email: info@wnpa.org or visit www.wnpa.org

Edited by Derek Gallagher
Design by Boelts/Stratford Associates, Tucson
Photography by Ken Howie
Electronic prepress preparation by Color Masters
Printed by Imago in China

Most of us learn about food and cooking from our parents. The food we ate as youngsters is what we feel most comfortable with. However, lately more and more people are becoming exposed to a wider variety of different cuisines. Through experimentation, along with good old trial and error, we find exciting new tastes to enjoy. One of the most delightful food styles now extremely popular throughout the United States has its roots in the rich, centuries-old cultures of Mexico and American Indians.

Records from the early Spanish campaign to conquer the New World reveal in detail what the Aztecs living in the verdant central valley of Mesoamerica cooked and ate. They had an abundance of fish, turkey, corn (maize), squash, eggplant, jícama, avocados, tomatoes, chocolate, and a wide variety of both beans and chiles. Some of what we eat in the Southwest today is much like many of the dishes served in the court of Montezuma. The arrival of the Spanish conquistadors and missionaries, who introduced wheat, goats, pigs, cattle and sheep to the New World, changed many of the food habits of the native population. The resulting cuisine remained very much the same even after Mexico's independence from Spain in 1821, and the portions of the American Southwest colonized by Spain still boast a strong link with this heritage.

Along with beef, pork, lard, milk, butter, and cheese the Spaniards also transported their methods and manner of preparing food. The mingling of foods and the eventual cooperation between the natives and the Spanish created an inventive, elegant, more complex style of cooking.

When the Spanish invaders pursued their conquest further north they found the Pueblo Indians just north of what is now Mexico struggling to grow vegetables on the rugged, often intimidating terrain. They had inhabited this area for at least 2,000 years and their diet consisted of wild game and vegetables, including corn and a wide variety of beans, squash, and cactus. The settlers soon adapted to the new diet, augmenting it with the beef and wheat they brought with them and introduced to the Indians.

Until the United States and Mexico established it there was, of course, no border and to this date the border, in terms of cuisine, remains fluid. The traditional way of cooking and eating has changed remarkably little even though it has been exposed to a great many other influences. The pioneers who braved the long trip along the Santa Fe trail from Kansas brought German, English, and French ingredients and their methods of food preparation. The arrival of the railroad made it possible to ship oysters, shrimp, and French cheeses into Texas,

Arizona, and New Mexico. Now television has brought a new wave of cooking into everyone's home. However, the cuisine of the Southwest is still patterned after the age-old Mexican/Indian style.

So what is "real" Southwestern food? A taco in Texas might be made from shredded beef and red chile, while a taco in New Mexico might be prepared with ground beef and green chile. An enchilada in a trendy Dallas restaurant might have crab in it, whereas the chef in an upscale Phoenix eatery might be equally as proud of his ground lamb enchiladas. A television chef from Santa Monica might tout the use of raw poblanos and a restaurateur promoting a book on a morning show might induce the host to eat shark fin tamales.

In Authentic Southwestern Cooking *we have tried to give you a taste of the cooking as exemplified by what cooks in the Southwest make and eat when there is no one watching and they are not trotting out the fine china for company. In this way we hope you will get the real feel of the area and be able to create some of these wonderful dishes in your kitchen.*

ANISE SEED: Very popular for use in Mexican and Southwestern cookies and pastries. They are especially good ground and used in biscochitos, a favorite Christmas treat.

ASADERO CHEESE: A white, semisoft cheese made from partially soured milk. This cheese is very popular in northern Mexico and in southwestern kitchens. You can substitute Monterey Jack or mozzarella or a combination of these two cheeses.

AVOCADOS: Avocados are used a great deal in Mexican and southwestern cooking. The best ones to use for the recipes in this book are the Mexican variety or Haas avocados, which usually are small, have a pebbly skin, and are dark green, almost black in color. Make sure the skin is not bruised and that they are just slightly soft to the touch. These are ready to eat.

BEANS: Beans have long been an important part of the diet of people living in the Southwest. Desert beans, such as MESQUITE beans, were a prominent food source, especially for the Indians. These beans were ground into flour or boiled to make a flavorful broth.

BLACK BEANS (frijoles negros), sometimes called black turtle beans, are native to the Yucatan. Black beans, with their creamy white interior, have a meaty texture and a hearty, smoky flavor and are a pleasant addition to many Southwestern dishes.

ANASAZI BEANS, cultivated by the Anasazi Indians of the Southwest are one of the "heirloom" beans that are rapidly gaining in popularity. The ancestors of these beans have been found in the Anasazi cave dwellings of New Mexico and date back thousands of years. These cranberry red and white mottled beans add great taste and color to salads and chilis.

PINTO BEANS, with their irregular dark spots, were no doubt named after the pinto horse. This bean is high in iron and vitamin B. Pinto beans are a ubiquitous part of Southwestern cooking. Although other beans are steadily gaining in popularity, pinto beans remain a staple in southwestern cuisine.

BLUE CORN: Blue corn is one of the varieties of corn Pueblo Indians have grown in the Southwest for centuries. Blue corn has a stronger flavor than white or yellow corn. You can use it to make tortillas, corn chips, pancakes, cornbread, and dumplings.

CHILES: Chiles, native to South America and Mexico, come in a wide variety of shapes, sizes, colors, and heat intensity. The chile family includes peppers from the BELL PEPPER, which usually is not hot at all, to the HABANERO, which is extremely hot, ranking number ten on the heat scale used by most researchers and developers to test the potency of chiles.

Some of the widely used chiles in the Southwest (with their heat rankings) are: SERRANO, a fiery green chile (seven on the heat scale) 3 to 3-1/2 inches long; POBLANO, a dark green, almost purple black, thick fleshed chile (three on the heat scale); ÁRBOL, a dried, red chile resembling a rooster's beak (seven and a half to eight on the heat scale); and PEQUÍN, a tiny chile with a fierce bite (eight to eight and a half on the heat scale).

CAYENNE is a very hot, long, thin, red pepper. It is usually used ground in sauces and soups or to add a fiery zing to main courses or vegetable dishes. It is very hot, about eight on the heat scale, and a little goes a long way.

JALAPEÑOS are the most widely consumed chile in America. They are a short, oval-shaped chile usually dark green and about 2 to 2-1/2 inches long. Jalapeños run from mild to very hot. They are usually used raw, but can also be found canned and/or pickled. Chipotles are dried and smoked jalapeños.

LONG GREEN CHILES are large, thick-fleshed chiles that taper from 6 to 8 inches long. Varieties include Baker, Rio Grande, Sandia, New-Mex, Big Jim, Anaheim, California, and Hatch Green Chile. The color of these chiles ranges from a light yellow-green to a vivid "grass" green. If left on the vine they turn red and when dried make the ground red chile used in the recipes in this book. Green chile is best when freshly roasted, and peeled. To roast the chile place on a rack over an open gas flame or on a charcoal grill. Or place on an oven rack and bake at 400 degrees or place under the broiler. Roast the chiles until the skin blisters and begins to blacken but doesn't burn through to the flesh of the chile.

After the chiles are roasted spread them out on a table covered with a damp towel or newspaper and place a wet towel over them and let them sit for a few minutes. This will help you remove the skins.

Then, using rubber gloves, remove the skins from the chiles and let them cool. You can keep them in plastic storage bags in the refrigerator up to two days or freeze them for later.

Leaving the seeds in or not is a personal preference. However, the seeds usually make the chile hotter and are hard for some people to digest. So some cooks remove most of the seeds. Green chiles can also be used canned, pickled, or dried. Green chiles range from sweet and mild to fire-breathing hot. The high content of vitamin C makes many people swear by chiles as the cure for everything from the common cold to ulcers.

RED CHILES are long green chiles that have stayed on the plant long enough to turn red. Long red chiles can be eaten fresh if roasted the same way as long green chile. However, they are usually dried and sold either in the pod or ground. When the recipes in this book call for ground red chile this is what is meant—not chili powder.

Everyone has a different tolerance to chile. If you are an uninitiated chile eater try a very little bit to start with and then increase the amount as you learn your tolerance level. ALL OF THE AMOUNTS OF CHILE CALLED FOR IN THE RECIPES IN THIS BOOK ARE TO BE USED ONLY AS A GUIDE AND YOU SHOULD ADJUST THE AMOUNTS IN ACCOR-DANCE WITH THE AMOUNT OF CHILE HEAT YOU CAN TOLERATE.

WARNING NOTE: When handling chile be sure and wear rubber gloves and/or wash your hands very well. Also do not touch your eyes or lips with your hands when handling chile.

CHILI POWDER: The chili powder sold in most supermarkets is a mixture of ground chiles, cumin, garlic powder, oregano, coriander, cloves, and allspice. This is not to be confused with the ground red chile called for in many of the recipes in this book That is made from ground chile pods and does not contain any additional ingredients.

CHORIZO: A Mexican sausage usually made from pork and highly seasoned with ground red chile. Most often served for breakfast with scrambled eggs or in a burrito. It is also wonderful with Heuvos Rancheros.

CILANTRO: Cilantro is the fresh leaves of the coriander plant. It is always used fresh, is very aromatic, and has a sharp pleasant, distinctive taste. Cilantro can be used without cooking in salads and salsas. It is also excellent in cooked dishes. However, when using cilantro in long-cooking dishes add it toward the end of the cooking process as it loses much of its flavor when cooked for a long time.

CORIANDER: Coriander usually refers to the seeds of the coriander plant which are dried and ground. Coriander adds pungency to soups and stews.

CORN: Corn is to Mexican cooking what wheat flour is to European-American cooking. Corn is used in an infinite number of ways, including dried and ground into flour. Ground corn flour is then made into tortillas, a staple in the Mexican diet much like sliced white bread is in the United States.

Corn is also used fresh or dried in a variety of stews, soups, and mixed vegetable dishes. Corn processed to make hominy is extremely popular in the Southwest, especially during the holidays. Hominy is the main ingredient in a dish called posole or pozole, which is also the Spanish name for the hominy itself.

CORN HUSKS: Corn husks are used in Mexico and the Southwest as a wrapper to cook food in. They are most commonly used to make tamales. The husks are soaked in warm water, the ingredients are placed on them, and the husks are folded to hold in the filling then tightly placed in a steamer and steamed.

COTIJA CHEESE: A dry, crumbly aged cheese with a sharp, somewhat salty flavor. This cheese does not melt well but makes a great topping for enchiladas, tacos, or refried beans.

CUMIN (comino): A spice from the dried fruit of a plant in the parsley family. Used in Middle Eastern, North African, and Mexican cuisines this robust spice with a nutty flavor is a must, used ground, in southwestern cooking and gives zip to chilis, stews, soups, beans, and salsas.

HOMINY: Kernels of corn soaked in a slaked lime solution produces hominy (posole or pozole in Spanish). Available both frozen and canned, hominy is the basis for stews, chilis, and soups and is the main ingredient in the dish also called posole.

JÍCAMA: A root vegetable most often eaten raw. Great for salads and salsas, it has a consistency similar to a raw turnip and tastes like a cross between a water chestnut and a crisp, tart apple.

LARD: Although it has long been the most widely used fat in Mexican cooking it is now at the top of the "foodies" list as a definite "no-no." Used in moderation it is not any more dangerous than the rest of the saturated fats. Lard is indispensable in such dishes as biscochitos and is wonderful in refried beans. You can substitute vegetable oil in other dishes as I've indicated in the recipes.

MANGOES: This tropical fruit is a yellow-green that shades from pink to a dark red. The flesh of the mango is a rich, deep yellow around a large, very hard seed. The fruit makes great salsas and desserts. The juice of the mango in combination with liquors such as tequila and rum makes delicious cocktails.

MASA: Masa is made by cooking dried corn with a small amount of lime. The corn is then finely ground using a little water to make the process easier. Masa can be purchased in the refrigerated section of supermarkets or stores specializing in Latin American and Mexican food and is used to make tamales or gorditas. Dried masa is usually sold under the label Masa Harina.

MONTEREY JACK CHEESE: An easy melting, mild cheese with a buttery flavor. Excellent for making nachos, quesadillas, and enchiladas.

OREGANO: Oregano is one of the most popular herbs used in Mexican and southwestern cooking. Mexican oregano has a milder, sweeter flavor and originates from a different family than Greek oregano. You can use fresh or ground oregano although dried, crushed oregano works best in most southwestern recipes.

PECANS: Pecans are grown all over the Southwest. They contain approximately 70 percent oil, more than most other nuts. Although when one thinks of pecans they most often think of pies, pecans are also used in salads, meat dishes, and other desserts, including candy. They make wonderful appetizers sautéed with garlic and red chile.

PIÑON NUTS: Piñon nuts grow in the high desert mesas of the Southwest and have a delicate, nutty flavor. Because they grow in limited areas and are hard to gather and shell they are expensive. If you can't find southwestern piñons you can substitute Italian or Greek pine nuts for them.

TABASCO SAUCE: A hot pepper sauce made in Louisiana by mashing and fermenting the tabasco chile with salt and vinegar. Although you can substitute other hot pepper sauces I find that Tabasco Sauce gives a rich flavor to many dishes.

TOMATILLOS: Although at first glance they look like a small green tomato, tomatillos are members of a separate family. Tomatillos are covered with a brown-beige husk and have a sharp, acidic taste that provides a unique tang to cooked salsas.

TORTILLAS: A round, flat bread made of corn for centuries in Mexico and most certainly originally used as eating utensils to scoop the food into the mouth. Flour tortillas made from wheat are a relatively new development and are usually larger than corn tortillas. They are most often used to make burritos or served warm on the side with many Mexican dishes. Corn tortillas, most often 5 inches in diameter, are commonly made from yellow or white corn, although, in recent years, it has become more and more popular to make them with blue corn. Corn tortillas are used in a variety of dishes including enchiladas, tacos, and soups. They are not eaten directly from the package but have to be lightly sauteed to soften or fried to make them crisp. They can also be used in a recipe where all the ingredients are cooked with the tortillas such as green enchilada casserole.

Flour tortillas are commonly served warm with a variety of southwestern dishes and take the place of bread. To warm the tortillas in a conventional oven, stack them on a damp dish towel then wrap tightly in aluminum foil and heat for 15 minutes in a 350 degree oven and serve at once.

TORTILLA SOUP

Tortilla soup has long been the way southwestern cooks used day-old corn tortillas by lightly frying and using them in this delectable soup. However, if you do not have any leftover tortillas, store-bought tortilla chips work just as well.

3	tablespoons olive oil
1	yellow onion, chopped
1	clove garlic, minced
2	large, ripe, red tomatoes, peeled and coarsely chopped
6	cups chicken stock or broth
1	tablespoon chopped cilantro
2	whole chicken breasts, skinned, boned, cooked, and cut into bite-size pieces
1/2	teaspoon salt
1/2	teaspoon freshly ground black pepper
1	jalapeño, seeded and diced
2	cups tortilla chips
6	tablespoons Monterey Jack cheese, grated
1	cup black olives, sliced

Sauté the garlic and onion in the olive oil until the onion is soft. Spoon the onion and garlic into a blender with the tomatoes, 1 cup of the chicken stock, and cilantro and blend until smooth. Pour the mixture into a saucepan, stir in the rest of the chicken stock, cooked chicken, salt, black pepper, and jalapeño and cook over medium heat until heated through.

Coarsely crumble the tortilla chips into the bottoms of individual soup bowls, pour the soup over the chips, sprinkle the cheese and olives on top, and serve at once.

Serves 6 to 8.

FESTIVE POSOLE

"Posole" or "pozole" is the Spanish word for hominy.

Hominy or posole is corn that has been processed by combining the corn kernels with a pickling agent and then cooking until they are tender.

In the Southwest you can buy frozen hominy and the canned variety is readily available throughout the country.

In southwestern cooking the term posole has carried over to mean a stew made with pork and spices and served with a red chile sauce on the side that can be spooned over the top of the posole. This is traditionally served on Christmas Eve and/or at New Year's celebrations.

2	tablespoons vegetable oil
1	large yellow onion, chopped
4	cloves garlic, minced
1	pound lean pork, cut into bite-size pieces
1	teaspoon freshly ground black pepper
1	teaspoon salt
1	tablespoon chopped fresh parsley
1	teaspoon chopped cilantro
1	teaspoon dried oregano, crushed
1	teaspoon ground cumin
2	tablespoons red chile flakes
4	cups chicken stock or broth
4	cups water
1	large can (#10) white hominy with the juice

Heat the oil in a large, heavy pot and sauté the onion, garlic, and pork until the pork is lightly browned. Add the pepper, salt, parsley, cilantro, oregano, cumin, red chile flakes, chicken stock, and water, cover and simmer over low heat for one hour. Add the hominy with the liquid from the can and continue cooking for one more hour, stirring occasionally over low heat. Add more water if necessary.

Serve with Basic Red Chile Sauce (recipe on page 21) on the side.

Serves 6 to 8.

Festive Posole

SOPA DE ALBÓNDIGAS (Meatball Soup)

Sopa de Albóndigas is one of the most familiar recipes in the kitchens of Spain. The meatballs were made from any meat the cook could find or had on hand, including pork, beef, chicken, or turkey, and was a great way to stretch a small amount of meat. Near the coast the meatballs are often made from fish or seafood, shrimp being one of the most popular.

The Spaniards brought the tradition of this soup with them to the Americas and it has become a favorite in homes and restaurants in both Mexico and the Southwest. It is often made and served when the hosts are expecting a large crowd such as on the Feast of Guadalupe.

For the Meatballs:

1	pound lean ground beef
2	cloves garlic, minced
1/2	teaspoon ground red chile
1/2	teaspoon salt
1/2	teaspoon freshly ground black pepper
1	cup dry bread crumbs
1	egg
1/2	yellow onion, finely chopped

For the Soup:

2	tablespoons olive oil
1/2	yellow onion, chopped
3	medium-size carrots, thinly sliced
1	tablespoon chopped fresh parsley
1	teaspoon dried oregano, crushed
2	ripe, red tomatoes, peeled and coarsely chopped
4	cups beef stock or broth
2	cups water
1	bay leaf

To make the Meatballs:

Mix together the ground beef, salt, chile, oregano, salt, pepper, and bread crumbs. Lightly beat the egg and stir into the mixture. Add the onion and mix well, then shape into small balls and reserve while you make the soup.

To make the Soup:

Pour the oil in a large soup pot and sauté the onion for 2 to 3 minutes, add the carrots, parsley, oregano, and tomatoes and sauté for 3 to 4 more minutes. Add the beef stock, water, and bay leaf and bring to a boil.

Add the meatballs, a few at a time, so that the boiling remains constant. After all the meatballs are in, reduce the heat, cover, and simmer for 30 minutes. Remove the bay leaf and serve hot with warm flour tortillas.

Serves 4 to 6.

CHICKEN, CORN, AND CHILE CHOWDER

4	tablespoons olive oil
1	large yellow onion, chopped
2	ribs celery, finely chopped
2	cups corn, cut off the cob, or frozen
2	cups cooked chicken, boned, skin removed, and diced
2	long green chiles, roasted, peeled, seeded, and chopped
1/2	teaspoon ground black pepper
2	dashes Tabasco Sauce
1	clove garlic, minced
2	cups chicken stock or broth
1	cup half and half

Heat the oil in a saucepan, add the onion, garlic, and celery and sauté until limp. Stir in the corn, cooked chicken, green chile, Tabasco Sauce, and chicken stock. Cook over low heat until warmed through, add the half and half and continue cooking until hot—but do not let boil.

Serves 6 as a first course or 4 as a main course.

CALDO

Caldo has many meanings in Spanish including "broth" or "stock," and it was the Spaniards who introduced to the Indians of Mexico the method of cooking foods in liquid.

Over a time Mexican and southwestern cooks started adding all manner of meat and vegetables to the simple clear broths they kept simmering on the back of the stove. In many areas of the Southwest the word "caldo" has now come to mean a clear soup or broth filled with chunks of meat and large pieces of vegetables. It is very often served with rice on the side and when served with the traditional bolillos (hard rolls) makes a complete, filling meal.

2	cups cooked roast beef, cut into bite-size pieces
4	potatoes, peeled and quartered
1	large yellow onion, quartered
3	carrots, peeled and sliced 2 inches long
2	turnips, peeled and quartered
1	head cabbage, coarsely chopped
2	ears fresh corn, sliced into 2-inch rounds
3	cups chicken stock or broth
3	cups water
1	teaspoon salt
1	teaspoon freshly ground black pepper
1	lime, quartered
1	tablespoon chopped cilantro
2	jalapeños, seeded and diced
	Cooked white rice

Place all the ingredients except the lime, cilantro, jalapeños, and rice into a large soup pot and simmer over medium heat for 1 hour.

Ladle into large soup bowls and top with a sprinkling of cilantro and jalapeño. Serve with a wedge of lime on the side and a bowl of hot cooked rice.

Serves 4.

Caldo

CHILLED SQUASH SOUP WITH SPRING ONIONS

Squash was an important food source for the Indians of the Southwest. The versatile vegetable was baked and then eaten hot or cold or chopped and put into stews. More tender summer squashes were boiled and used in soups. Squash, like corn, was also of ceremonial significance to American Indians.

During the heat of the summer nothing is easier to make and more refreshing to eat than cold soups. This soup is especially good when made a few hours ahead and chilled in the refrigerator. I like making it in the cool morning hours and serving it for lunch.

1	tablespoons olive oil
2	cloves garlic, minced
1/2	yellow onion, peeled and coarsely chopped
4	medium size yellow crookneck squash, well-washed, ends cut off, sliced
2	-inch-long lemon peel
1	tablespoon chopped fresh parsley
1	teaspoon salt
1	cup chicken stock or broth
1	(32-ounce) container non-fat plain yogurt
1/8	teaspoon ground cayenne pepper
2	green (spring) onions, chopped with some of the green portion

Place the oil in a non-stick frying pan and lightly sauté the garlic and onion for 2 to 3 minutes, add the squash and sauté for 3 to 4 minutes more. Stir in the lemon peel, parsley, salt, and chicken stock, cover and cook over low heat for 8 to 10 minutes or until the squash is tender.

Let cool for a few minutes, remove the lemon peel, then place the squash mixture in a blender or food processor and blend or process until smooth. Chill in the refrigerator for at least a half hour.

Add the yogurt and cayenne to the squash mixture and blend until smooth. Pour into a glass bowl or plastic pitcher and chill in the refrigerator for 4 to 6 hours. Pour the soup into glass soup bowls, garnish with the chopped green onions, and serve at once.

Serves 4 to 6.

Chilled Squash Soup
with Spring Onions

GREEN CHILE STEW

A cross between a soup and chili, there are as many variations of this dish as there are cooks. You can make it with chunks of beef, pork, or lamb. It is also commonly made with ground beef, ground pork, or a combination of these two meats.

Long green chiles such as Hatch Green Chile give this dish its rich, distinctive flavor. Predicate the amount of chiles you use on your tolerance to the heat of the chile.

3 to 4	tablespoons olive oil
2	cloves garlic, minced
1	large yellow onion, chopped
1	pound lean ground beef
1/2	pound ground pork
3	cups chicken stock or broth
3	cups water
6	mild long green chiles, roasted, peeled, seeded, and chopped
4	large potatoes, peeled and diced
2	cups corn, cut off the cob or frozen
1	teaspoon freshly ground black pepper
1	teaspoon dried, crushed oregano
1/2	teaspoon ground cumin
1	tablespoon finely chopped fresh parsley
1	teaspoon salt

Heat the oil in a large pot and sauté the garlic and onions for 3 to 4 minutes. Add the ground beef and pork and cook, stirring, until cooked through. Add the rest of the ingredients and cook over low heat for approximately 1 hour or until meat and potatoes are done.

Serves 6 to 8.

BASIC RED CHILE SAUCE

You can use this classic red chile sauce for enchiladas, huevos rancheros, and as an accompaniment to posole.

Although many purists do not like tomato added to this sauce I feel that a touch of tomato gives more body to the sauce.

15 to 20	dried mild red chile pods
	(or to your taste—you can use hot, if you prefer)
4 to 5	cups water
2	tablespoons vegetable oil
2	tablespoons all-purpose flour
1	teaspoon ground cumin
1	teaspoon salt
1	tablespoon tomato paste (optional)

Wash the chile pods and remove the stems and place in a heavy saucepan, add the water, and bring to a boil. Lower the heat and cook for approximately 15 minutes. Let cool, then spoon some of the chile pods into a blender, covering with water until the blender is no more than half full. Pulse until blended, then strain through a sieve.

Repeat the process until all the chile pods are blended. Heat the oil in a heavy saucepan, stir in the flour, and let cook, over high heat, until the flour just begins to turn brown.

Stir in the red chile, cumin, salt, and tomato paste. Reduce the heat and simmer over low heat for 5 to 10 minutes.

Makes 5 to 6 cups.

NACHOS WITH TWO CHEESES, RED CHILE, AND PIÑON NUTS

This recipe uses Cheddar cheese, which melts easily, and the Mexican cheese, Cotija, a hard cheese that doesn't melt well but gives the nachos an extra zing when sprinkled on top just before serving.

12 to 16	round, flat corn tortilla chips
1	teaspoon ground red chile
12 to 16	teaspoons refried beans (see recipe on page 52)
1	cup shredded Cheddar cheese
1	cup shelled piñon nuts
1/4	cup grated Cotija or Parmesan cheese

Line a baking sheet with aluminum foil. Stir the ground red chile into the refried beans, then spread a teaspoon of refried beans on each tortilla chip, sprinkle with the Cheddar cheese, and a few piñon nuts.

Bake in a 325 degree oven and heat for 5 to 10 minutes or until the Cheddar cheese has melted. Sprinkle the Cotija cheese over the top while still hot and serve warm as an appetizer with Mexican beer.

Serves 3 to 4 as an appetizer.

Nachos with Two Cheeses,
Red Chile, and Piñon Nuts

PICO DE GALLO

Pico de Gallo translated from the Spanish means "rooster's beak." This salsa is so named because the jalapeño reaches out and bites you just like a rooster if you get too close.

1	small white onion, finely chopped
2	cloves garlic, minced
2	ripe, red tomatoes, peeled and diced
2	jalapeños, seeded and chopped, or to your taste
1	tablespoon chopped cilantro
	Juice of 2 limes
2	teaspoons olive oil

Place the chopped onion, garlic, tomatoes, and jalapeño in a glass bowl. Add the cilantro, lime juice, and oil and lightly stir. Cover and refrigerate 1 hour before serving. This is best eaten the day it's prepared as it does not store well.

Makes approximately 1 cup.

SALSA FRESCA

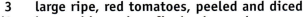

Everyone in the Southwest has a favorite salsa recipe.

While cooked salsas are popular condiments, salsas made with fresh ingredients give zip and interest to any meal. Serve this salsa with chips or assorted raw vegetables including sliced jícama. Also makes an excellent accompaniment to grilled chicken or fish.

3	large ripe, red tomatoes, peeled and diced
1/2	large white onion, finely chopped
4	mild, long green chiles, roasted, peeled, seeded, and chopped
1	clove garlic, minced
2	tablespoons olive oil
1	tablespoon lemon juice
1	tablespoon chopped cilantro
1/2	teaspoon salt
1/2	teaspoon freshly ground black pepper
1/4	teaspoon dried, crushed oregano

Mix all the ingredients together and chill for a half hour before serving. Serve at once as it does not store well.

Makes approximately 2 cups.

ENSALADA GUACAMOLE (Avocado Salad)

The Indians of Mexico were using not only the flesh of the avocado but the leaves of the tree and the pit as well long before Cortez landed on their shores. The toasted leaves were added to stews much like we would add a bay leaf today, the pit was grated and small amounts used in dishes such as enchiladas, and, of course, the flesh was sliced or mashed and added to any number of recipes, including tostadas and salsas.

Avocados will darken very rapidly after being peeled. Squeeze a little lemon juice over the flesh if you are serving them sliced or incorporate the lemon juice into the recipe when serving them mashed.

2	large avocados, peeled, pitted, and mashed
1	small ripe, red tomato, diced
1	clove garlic, minced
1/2	small red onion, finely diced
1/2	teaspoon salt
1	tablespoon lemon juice
	Dash of Tabasco Sauce
	Lettuce leaves
	Sliced tomatoes
	Sliced cucumbers
	Tortilla chips

Mix the mashed avocados, diced tomato, garlic, onion, salt, lemon juice, and Tabasco Sauce together in a small bowl. Mound on lettuce leaves, surround with sliced tomatoes and sliced cucumbers.

Serve with tortilla chips stuck into the edges.

Serves 2 to 4 as an appetizer.

Ensalada Guacamole

CHILE VERDE (Green Chile Sauce)

One can hear the familiar question "red or green" in restaurants throughout the Southwest. There are people who will only eat red chile sauce on their enchiladas and burritos and there are those who are addicted to green chile sauce.

If the restaurant patron is undecided the follow-up question to the waiter may be "which is hottest?" to determine their selection. This recipe suggests mild green chiles, but use your own "chile thermometer" as your guide when preparing this tasty sauce.

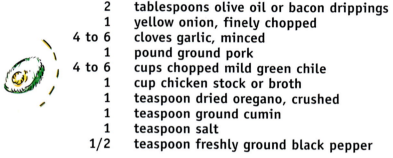

2	tablespoons olive oil or bacon drippings
1	yellow onion, finely chopped
4 to 6	cloves garlic, minced
1	pound ground pork
4 to 6	cups chopped mild green chile
1	cup chicken stock or broth
1	teaspoon dried oregano, crushed
1	teaspoon ground cumin
1	teaspoon salt
1/2	teaspoon freshly ground black pepper

Heat the oil in a heavy frying pan and sauté the onion and garlic for 2 to 3 minutes. Stir in the pork and sauté for 4 to 5 minutes. Add the chile, chicken stock, oregano, cumin, salt, and pepper and cook, over low heat for 20 minutes or until the flavors are well blended.

Makes 4 to 6 cups.

GREEN CHILE–TOMATILLO SALSA

In pre-Columbian Mexico the tomatillo was most likely consumed in greater quantities than red tomatoes. Although often mistaken for green tomatoes and even sometimes called "tomates verdes," tomatillos are actually members of the same botanical family as gooseberries and not related to the tomato.

The wonderful sharp taste of tomatillos coupled with green chile makes a superb salsa for grilled fish or chicken.

2	tablespoons olive oil
1/2	yellow onion, finely chopped
1	clove garlic, finely minced
6 to 8	tomatillos, husks removed, coarsely chopped
4	mild, long green chiles, roasted, peeled, seeded, and chopped
1/4	cup water
2	teaspoons chopped cilantro
1/2	teaspoon salt
1/2	teaspoon freshly ground black pepper

Pour the oil in a non-stick saucepan and sauté the onion and garlic for 3 to 4 minutes. Add the tomatillos, chiles, and water and cook over low heat for 10 minutes. Remove from the heat and let cool, then stir in the cilantro, salt, and pepper.

Chill in the refrigerator for a least an hour before serving.

Makes approximately 2 cups.

QUESADILLAS WITH MONTEREY JACK CHEESE AND ROSEMARY

Quesadillas are a delightful appetizer or late night snack. They are made in several different ways, including open faced or folded flour tortillas with anything from just plain cheese to a combination of several cheeses adorned with a variety of other ingredients.

1/2	pound Monterey Jack (or asadero) cheese, sliced
2	green onions, seeded and chopped
2	jalapeños, seeded and chopped
1	tablespoon chopped fresh rosemary
2	large flour tortillas

Place slices of cheese on the tortillas, sprinkle the onions, jalapeños, and rosemary over the cheese and place on a baking sheet in a 350 degree oven until the cheese melts. Remove from the oven, fold the tortillas in half, slice into 3 triangles, and serve at once.

Serves 2 to 4 as an appetizer.

Quesadillas with Monterey Jack
Cheese and Rosemary

CHICKEN TOSTADA SALAD WITH PICO DE GALLO

Tostadas can either be an appetizer or a whole meal by themselves. The tortillas are crisply fried and regularly served open faced, topped with refried beans, then chicken or meat, lettuce, cheese, and tomatoes. You can pile the ingredients as high as you'd like and the dish is as eye catching as it is tasty.

4	corn tortillas, fried until crisp and drained on paper towels
2	cups refried beans (see recipe on page 52)
2	cups cooked chicken, chopped
2	cups finely shredded lettuce
1	cup shredded Cheddar cheese
1	avocado, peeled, pitted, and chopped
2	tablespoons sour cream
1/2	cup chopped black olives
	Pico de Gallo (see recipe on page 24)

Spread 1/4 of the refried beans on each of the corn tortillas, then top with 1/4 of the chicken, 1/4 of the lettuce, 1/4 of the cheese, 1/4 of the avocado, and 1/4 of the sour cream.

Sprinkle the top of each with 1/4 of the black olives and serve with Pico de Gallo or a tablespoon of your favorite salsa.

Serves 2 as a main course.

Chicken Tostada Salad
with Pico de Gallo

TACOS

"Taco" in Spanish means, among other things, a bite or snack. Tacos no doubt came about long before forks when Meso-Americans used them to carry food from the serving vessel to their mouths. In Mexico, tacos are street food, sold everywhere as snacks or light meals by vendors from carts, much as hot dogs are in America.

Tacos are made with folded corn tortillas filled with meat, chicken, fish, or beans and topped with cheese, shredded lettuce, and chopped tomatoes. They are the Mexican equivalent of a sandwich.

You can make your own taco shells by rapidly frying corn tortillas in vegetable oil, draining them on paper towels, and folding the tortillas over so that they form a shell. The easiest thing, however, is to buy the taco shells ready made.

2	tablespoons vegetable oil
1/2	yellow onion, diced
1	clove garlic, minced
1	pound lean ground beef
1/2	teaspoon ground cumin
1/2	teaspoon salt
1/2	teaspoon freshly ground black pepper
12	taco shells
2	cups finely grated Cheddar cheese
2	cups shredded lettuce
2	ripe, red tomatoes, diced

Heat the oil in a frying pan, cook the onions and garlic for 2 to 3 minutes over medium heat, add the beef and cook, stirring with a fork until it is browned and crumbly. Spoon an equal portion of the meat and onion mixture into each taco shell, top with cheese, lettuce, and tomatoes. Serve with your favorite salsa or Pico de Gallo (see recipe on page 24).

Serves 4.

STACKED RED ENCHILADAS WITH CHEESE AND ONIONS

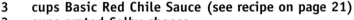

The trick to making great enchiladas is to lightly sauté the tortillas before assembling the enchiladas—but do not let the tortillas become crisp. Also be sure to put the chile sauce over the entire tortilla so that the edges do not dry out between making and serving the enchiladas.

3	cups Basic Red Chile Sauce (see recipe on page 21)
3	cups grated Colby cheese
1	large yellow onion, finely chopped
2	tablespoons vegetable oil
12	corn tortillas
1	tablespoon butter
4	eggs
	Shredded lettuce
1	ripe, red tomato, chopped

Heat the chile sauce over low heat. While it is heating warm the oil in a frying pan. Using tongs, dip each tortilla in the hot oil just long enough to soften it. DO NOT FRY! Place one tortilla on each of 4 plates. Spoon 2 tablespoons of the red chile sauce over it. Divide the onion and cheese on top of the sauce, then repeat the process with two more tortillas and pour the remaining sauce, in equal portions, over the top.

Place the plates in a warm oven to melt the cheese. While the cheese is melting, melt the butter in the frying pan you were using to warm the tortillas and fry the eggs. Place one egg on top of each enchilada. Surround the edges of the tortillas with shredded lettuce and chopped tomato and serve.

Serves 4.

INDIAN TACOS

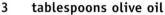

Indian tacos are a delectable mixture of ground beef, tomatoes, chile, onions, and cheese served on the traditional Indian Fry Bread. The name of the dish varies and is also called "Hopi Taco" or "Navajo Taco" depending on who is making it, but it is essentially the same dish.

3	tablespoons olive oil
1	onion, chopped
1	clove garlic, minced
1	teaspoon dried oregano, crushed
1	teaspoon ground cumin
1	pound lean ground beef
1	teaspoon red chile flakes
	Grated Cheddar or longhorn cheese
	Shredded lettuce
2	ripe, red tomatoes, diced
	Indian Fry Bread (recipe on page 56)

Sauté the onion, garlic and parsley in the olive oil for 3 to 4 minutes, then add the oregano, cumin, ground beef, and red chile flakes. Cook, stirring with a fork until the meat is brown and crumbled. Spoon some of the meat into the center of a piece of Indian Fry Bread. Spoon on your favorite salsa or the Green Chile Sauce (recipe on page 28). Top with grated cheese, shredded lettuce, and chopped tomatoes.

Serves 4 to 6.

Indian Tacos
with Indian Fry Bread

NEW MEXICO HUEVOS RANCHEROS

The Spaniards brought cattle to the New World early in the sixteenth century. Cattle raising, centered around haciendas in Mexico, made its way north and ranching then became an integral part of the Southwest's economy. The terrain is rough and the vegetation sparse; it takes many acres to feed a herd. Ranches are usually quite large, sometimes covering thousands or tens of thousands of acres. Cowhands have to make sure the herds stay together, have water, and move to the best grazing land. It is rough, appetite-building work. Ranch hands fortify themselves for the day with a hearty breakfast. Eggs served on tortillas topped with Mexican-style sausage and a spicy red chile sauce are a prime example.

2	tablespoons olive oil
1/2	white onion, finely chopped
1	clove garlic, minced
1	pound chorizo or pork sausage
3	cups Basic Red Chile Sauce (recipe on page 21)
	Vegetable oil
8	corn tortillas
4	tablespoons grated longhorn or Colby cheese
8	eggs
	Shredded lettuce
1	large ripe, red tomato, finely chopped
	Refried Beans (recipe on page 52)

Heat the 2 tablespoons of olive oil in a frying pan and cook the onion and garlic for 3 to 4 minutes. Add the chorizo or sausage to the pan and sauté until the chorizo is cooked through.

Heat the Basic Red Chile Sauce in a saucepan. Then, heat a small amount of vegetable oil in a frying pan and dip the tortillas, one at a time, with tongs, in the hot oil until they are limp. Quickly drain on paper towels. Place two tortillas on each plate. Spoon a couple tablespoons of the Basic Red Chile Sauce over each tortilla. Sprinkle equal amounts of sausage over the sauce. Drizzle the remaining sauce over the top, or to your taste. Sprinkle the cheese on top of the sauce and the sausage and place under the broiler 1 to 2 minutes or until the cheese melts.

Fry the eggs sunny-side up, or to your taste, and place an egg on each tortilla. Garnish with shredded lettuce and chopped tomato. Serve with Refried Beans on the side.

Serves 4.

New Mexico Huevos Rancheros

GREEN CHILE ENCHILADAS

To many residents of the Southwest enchiladas are the reigning monarchs in the food world. Enchilada in Spanish means "to sauce with chile" and there are many variations including stacked corn tortillas with a red sauce (see recipe on page 21) and these baked green chile enchiladas.

Although we use chicken here, you can use only cheese or cheese and onion or cooked ground or shredded beef.

12	corn tortillas
	Vegetable oil
4	cups cooked, skinned, and boned chicken breasts, diced
1-1/2	cups grated Monterey Jack cheese
1/2	medium yellow onion, chopped
2	tablespoons butter
2	tablespoons all-purpose flour
1	cup chicken stock or broth
2	cups milk
1/2	teaspoon garlic powder
1/4	teaspoon freshly ground black pepper
1	teaspoon ground cumin
2	mild long green chiles, roasted, peeled, seeded, and chopped
1-1/2	cups grated Cheddar cheese

Heat just enough vegetable oil in a frying pan to lightly coat each tortilla and turn each tortilla in the hot oil just until soft. Equally divide the chicken, Monterey Jack cheese, and onion and place on each tortilla. Roll up the tortillas and place in a lightly greased 9 X 13-inch glass baking dish.

Melt the butter in a cast iron skillet, briskly stir in the flour, and cook over medium heat for 1 to 2 minutes, stirring or whisking constantly. Then add the chicken stock and stir well.

Add the milk, garlic powder, cumin, and green chile to the pan, bring it to a rolling boil, then reduce the heat and cook over low heat until warmed, stirring to blend everything. Pour the sauce over the rolled tortillas. Sprinkle with the grated Cheddar cheese and bake in a 325 degree oven for 30 minutes or until the casserole is hot and bubbly. Serve at once.

Serves 4 to 6.

EGG, GREEN CHILE, AND BEAN BURRITOS

Legend has it that the burrito was a practical way for Mexicans who worked in the fields to carry their lunch. Their labors might be some distance from their houses, making it impossible to go home for lunch. Since sliced white bread was unheard of they cleverly mixed chopped or shredded meat with potatoes, cheese, chile, and whatever else they had and rolled it up in a tortilla. The tortilla became the "burro" to carry the filling, thus inspiring the name "burrito."

3	eggs
1/4	teaspoon salt
2	teaspoons butter
2	green onions, chopped with some of the tops
1	mild long green chile, roasted, peeled, seeded, and chopped
1	cup Refried Beans (see recipe on page 52)
2	flour tortillas
1	cup grated Colby cheese

Lightly beat the eggs, then add the salt. Melt the butter in a frying pan, pour in the eggs, add the green onion and chile and lightly scramble until done.

Heat the flour tortillas in an oven or a dry skillet just until they are warmed through. Spoon 1/2 of the Refried Beans down the middle of each tortilla, divide the scrambled eggs in half, and place over the beans. Sprinkle the grated cheese on top of the egg, fold each end in, then roll up the tortillas and serve warm.

Serves 2.

CHICKEN FAJITAS

The Spanish word "fajita" means a sash or little belt. Originally fajitas were made from skirt steaks and hence the name. Now, however, fajitas are made from a variety of meats, one of the most popular being chicken.

I think of fajitas as a burrito wearing a party hat. The ingredients are usually fancier, including avocado, sour cream, and pico de gallo. And as a variation on this recipe you can serve all the ingredients in separate bowls and let your guests assemble their own fajitas, selecting how much they want of each offering.

4	boneless, skinless chicken breasts, cut in 1 x 1 & 1/2-inch strips
1/2	cup fajita marinade or Italian salad dressing
1/4	cup chopped cilantro
1	tablespoon lemon juice
1	clove garlic, minced
3	tablespoons olive oil
2	medium green bell peppers, cut into strips
1	medium red bell pepper, cut into strips
1	yellow onion, cut into strips
1	avocado, peeled, pitted, and cut into long strips
	Sour cream
	Grated Cheddar cheese
	Pico de Gallo (recipe on page 24)
	Warmed flour tortillas

Put the chicken strips in a glass bowl, cover with the fajita marinade or Italian dressing, cilantro, lemon juice, and garlic. Cover and marinate in the refrigerator for at least 4 hours.

Heat the olive oil in a frying pan and sauté the peppers and onion until crisp-tender. Drain the chicken and grill over hot coals or sauté in olive oil in a frying pan. Divide the chicken, peppers, and onions and place on top of warmed flour tortillas. Top with avocado strips and serve with small bowls of sour cream, grated cheese, and Pico de Gallo so that people can top the fajitas to their taste.

Serves 4.

Chicken Fajitas

RED CHILE TAMALES

Tamales are a traditional southwestern favorite especially around the holidays. Since masa (corn meal) was plentiful in the area, and meat often scarce— tamales were a filling main course using a small amount of meat such as pork for flavoring. Spiced with red or green chile, tamales are customarily cooked in corn husks, which are available in markets specializing in Mexican food.

Masa Harina, called for in this recipe, is a prepared combination of corn that has been treated with lime water and ground corn flour. You can find this in supermarkets or specialty stores that specialize in southwestern food.

Because tamales are time consuming to make often several people will gather just before special events, such as Christmas or New Years, to make and assemble the tamales and enjoy each other's company.

To prepare the red chile–meat filling:

1	pound boneless pork, cut into small cubes
2	tablespoons vegetable oil
2	tablespoons all-purpose flour
1	yellow onion, finely chopped
2	cloves garlic, minced
2	cups Basic Red Chile Sauce (see recipe on page 21)
1	teaspoon salt
1	teaspoon dried oregano, crushed
1	teaspoon ground cumin

Coat the pork cubes with flour. Heat the oil in a large frying pan and sauté the pork, onion, and garlic until the meat has browned. Add the chile sauce, salt, oregano, and cumin and cook, covered, over very low heat for 1 hour or until the pork falls apart. Then, mash the pork to make a thick paste.

To make the dough:

1	cup lard or vegetable shortening
1	teaspoon salt
5	cups Masa Harina
1	tablespoon baking soda
3	cups warm water (add more if necessary to make the dough pliable)

Beat the lard and salt until light and fluffy. Add Masa Harina, soda, and warm water and mix together well. Add more water if necessary to make the dough sticky, so it will adhere to corn husks.

To assemble the tamales:
          24   corn husks
                Water

Soak corn husks in warm water until they are soft and pliable. Place the corn husks in the palm of your hand, holding the base of the husk with your thumb. Place a tablespoon of the dough in the center and using the back of a spoon gently spread the dough out to the edges so that it is about 1/2 inch thick. Put a tablespoon of the red chile–meat filling in the center, fold the 2 sides together into thirds, then the top and bottom to make a rectangle. Stand the tamales on end, packing them close enough together so that the tamales do not come unwrapped, on a rack in a steamer over hot water. Cover and steam over medium heat for 1 hour. Check the tamales several times and add boiling hot water, if necessary, as they cook.

The tamales are done when they easily pull away from the husks. You can either serve at once or store them in the refrigerator for a day or two until ready to serve and warm them in the microwave. They also freeze well.

Remove the husks just before serving.

Makes approximately 2 dozen tamales.

MARGARITA SHRIMP

Margarita, the drink, is a favorite among southwesterners. The same makings that go into the drink also make a wonderful sauce in which to cook shrimp or chicken.

I prefer using a gold or aged tequila for the recipe. Remember the motto, "the better the tequila, the better the dish."

2	tablespoons olive oil
2	cloves garlic, minced
1	tablespoon chopped fresh parsley
24	large shrimp, shelled and deveined
1	tablespoon lime juice
2	tablespoons tequila
1	tablespoon orange-flavored liqueur
2	tablespoons butter

Heat the oil in a large frying pan, stir in the garlic, parsley, and shrimp and sauté for 5 minutes. Add the lime juice, tequila, and orange liqueur and continue cooking, stirring occasionally for 3 to 4 minutes or until the shrimp turn a pink color and are done. Stir in the butter until it melts, then serve over white rice.

Serves 4.

CHILE RELLENOS (Stuffed Green Chiles)

Chile relleno in Spanish literally means "stuffed chile." Long green New Mexico chiles are the best for stuffing. However, Anaheim and poblano chiles also work well. In most southwestern homes and restaurants the chiles are stuffed with cheese, but let your imagination be your guide and experiment with using cooked shrimp, ground pork, or finely chopped, sautéed vegetables such as zucchini mixed with the cheese.

8	long, mild green chiles, roasted, and peeled, with the stems on
8	pieces of Colby cheese cut into long strips just smaller than the chiles
1/2	cup all-purpose flour
1	teaspoon paprika
1/2	teaspoon garlic powder
	Pinch of baking soda
3 to 4	eggs, well beaten
2 to 3	cups vegetable oil for deep fat frying

Slit the chiles lengthwise in the middle, being careful not to cut the top or the bottom of the chiles. Remove the seeds. Place a piece of cheese inside each chile and fold one edge of the opening into the other to form a seal.

Mix the flour, paprika, garlic powder, and baking soda together. Dip the chiles in the beaten egg, then coat with the flour mixture, and dip in the egg again. Heat the oil in a large heavy pot or a deep fat fryer. Fry the chiles in the hot oil until golden brown. Place on paper towels to absorb any excess oil and serve at once with Traditional Red Rice (recipe on page 48) and Refried Beans (recipe on page 52).

Serves 4 to 6.

TRADITIONAL RED RICE

Rice was brought to the New World by the Spaniards along with so many other ingredients now integral to Southwestern cooking. This rice dish, flavored with onion, bell pepper, and tomato, is standard fare on most southwestern restaurant menus. This is the real thing and a wonderful complement to enchiladas, chile rellenos, tacos, or burritos.

3	tablespoons olive oil
1	large yellow onion, diced
1	green bell pepper, seeded, membranes removed, and diced
1	cup medium grain white rice
1	clove garlic, minced
2	ripe, red tomatoes, peeled and diced
1	can (8 oz.) tomato sauce
2	cups water
1/2	teaspoon salt

Heat the oil in a heavy pan, sauté the onion and bell pepper, then stir in the rice and sauté until lightly colored. Add the garlic and stir. Add the tomatoes, tomato sauce, water, and salt. Cover, turn the heat down to a very low simmer, and cook for 20 minutes. Check the rice 2 or 3 times during the cooking process and stir with a fork each time.

Serves 4 to 6.

RED CHILE POTATOES

Although they have spread throughout the cuisines of the world, potatoes are a native American plant used by many indigenous people. When you add onion and some flavorful New Mexico red chile to them you have a superb side dish you will be hard pressed to pass up.

2	tablespoons butter
3	tablespoons olive oil
1	medium onion, cut in half lengthwise and sliced
4	large white potatoes, thinly sliced
1/2	teaspoon salt
1	teaspoon freshly ground black pepper
1	teaspoon ground mild New Mexico red chile, or to taste

Melt butter in a frying pan, add olive oil, and sauté the onion for 2 to 3 minutes. Add the potatoes, salt, pepper, and ground red chile. Sauté, for 20 to 30 minutes or until the potatoes are done through and lightly browned.

Serves 4 to 6.

CALABACITAS (Squash Casserole)

- - - - - - - - - - - - - - - - - - -

Squash is native to the Americas and the Pueblo Indians grew many different varieties and even used the squash blossoms. This recipe couples two of the most important of Indian foods, corn and squash, with tomatoes, onions, and chile to make a truly memorable side dish.

2	tablespoons butter
1	small yellow onion, chopped
2	cloves garlic, minced
1	green bell pepper, seeded and chopped
2	medium yellow crookneck squash
2	Indian squash or zucchini
1	ripe, red tomato, peeled and chopped
1-1/2	cups corn kernels, cut off the cob or frozen
1	mild, long green chile, roasted, peeled, seeded, and chopped
1/4	teaspoon dried oregano, crushed
1/2	teaspoon ground cumin
1/4	teaspoon freshly ground black pepper
1	cup grated Cheddar cheese

Preheat oven to 325 degrees. Melt the butter in a heavy skillet and sauté the onion, garlic, and bell pepper over medium heat for 4 to 5 minutes. Cut the squash into 1/4-inch slices and sauté for 4 to 5 more minutes. Add the tomatoes, corn, chile, salt, oregano, cumin, and black pepper and stir.

Spoon the squash-corn mixture into a lightly greased baking glass dish, sprinkle the cheese on top, and bake in a 325 degree oven for 30 minutes.

Serves 4 to 6.

NEW MEXICO–STYLE PINTO BEANS

Pinto beans are a staple of southwestern cooking. Since they grow easily in semi-arid climates, they were most likely introduced by the Spanish missionaries who transplanted them from Central America. The pinto bean has been used for centuries in Mexico and the Southwest and to this day legions of cooks put on a pot of beans every morning to feed their families.

1	pound (approximately 2-1/2 cups) dry pinto beans
3	quarts water
1/2	cup ham, salt pork, or bacon, diced
2	cloves garlic, coarsely chopped
1	teaspoon New Mexico red chile flakes, optional
	Salt and freshly ground black pepper to taste

Wash the beans and pick them over, discarding any shriveled beans, pebbles, or any "floaters." Drain and discard the water, cover with new water, and soak the beans over night. The next morning, drain the beans again and place them in a large heavy pot or a crockpot.

Place the ham, salt pork, or bacon in a frying pan, cover with water, and bring to the boil. Instantly turn down the heat and let simmer 5 to 6 minutes to remove most of the salt as the salt will make the beans tough. Drain and add to the pot. Add the garlic, and chile flakes, if desired. Cover with water and bring to a boil, then reduce the heat and simmer for approximately 4 hours or until the beans are done. If you need more water add hot water not cold water to the pot.

If cooking the beans in a crockpot, follow the above steps but cook the beans on high for 1 hour, then reduce the heat to low and cook the beans for 4 more hours or until done.

Add salt and pepper to taste before serving.

Serves 8 to 10.

REFRIED BEANS

Refried beans are an extremely practical way southwestern cooks use leftover pinto beans. Many people do not think a Mexican-style meal is complete without a serving of refried beans and I know restaurant patrons who will walk out if the beans are not offered on the menu.

Traditionally lard or bacon drippings are used to season the beans. If you prefer a low-fat substitute use olive oil. But you'll need to add additional seasoning, such as a 1/2 teaspoon of salt.

A generous helping of grated cheese sprinkled over the top of the beans makes a terrific side dish for New Mexico Huevos Rancheros (recipe on page 38) or tacos.

2	tablespoons lard or bacon drippings
4	cups cooked pinto beans (can used canned)
1/2	cup of the juice the beans were cooked in
	Grated Cotijo or Cheddar cheese, optional

Heat the lard or bacon drippings in a heavy cast iron skillet, then add the beans and 1/2 cup of the juice the beans were cooked in. Cook the beans over high heat and using a potato masher, mash the beans as they cook adding more liquid, if necessary. When the beans become a thick paste turn the heat down to very low and simmer until ready to serve.

Season to taste with salt and pepper and sprinkle with grated cheese, if desired.

Serves 4 to 6.

GREEN CHILE AND CHEESE CORNBREAD

There is no doubt that cornbread is good. But the addition of mild green chile and cheese makes it outstanding. The trick to making great cornbread is to heat the oil in a cast iron skillet in a very hot (400 degree) oven, then pour in the batter and reduce the heat. This method produces a bread with a nice, dark brown crust and a soft, moist center.

1/2	cup vegetable oil, divided
1	cup yellow corn meal
1	cup all-purpose flour
1	teaspoon baking soda
1	teaspoon baking powder
1/4	teaspoon salt
1	egg
1	cup buttermilk
1	long, mild green chile, roasted, peeled, seeded, and chopped (or 1 jalapeño, seeded and chopped)
1	cup grated Cheddar cheese
1	cup whole kernel corn, cut off the cob or frozen

Preheat oven to 400 degrees.

Pour 1/4 cup of the oil into a cast iron skillet and place in a 400 degree oven to heat. While it is heating place the corn meal, flour, baking soda, baking powder, and salt in a bowl and stir. Add the milk, the remaining 1/4 cup of the oil, the egg, chile, corn, and cheese and mix well.

Pour the batter into the heated skillet, reduce the oven heat to 375 degrees, and bake for 30 minutes or until done through.

Serves 4 to 6.

CORN-CHILE PUDDING

This makes an excellent side dish with roast pork or venison. Also is a great addition to Thanksgiving dinner.

2	tablespoons butter
1/2	white onion, chopped
1	red bell pepper, membranes removed, seeded, and chopped
2	mild, long green chiles, roasted, peeled, seeded, and chopped
2	cups corn, cut off the cob or frozen
4	eggs
2	dashes Tabasco Sauce
1/2	teaspoon sugar
1/2	teaspoon salt
1/2	teaspoon freshly ground black pepper
1	cup milk
1	cup half and half
1/3	cup all-purpose flour
1/2	cup grated Cheddar cheese

Preheat oven to 325 degrees.

Melt the butter in a frying pan. Stir in the onion and bell pepper and cook for 2 to 3 minutes over low heat. Then add the green chiles and corn and cook for 3 to 4 minutes more. Lightly butter a 2-quart glass baking dish and spoon the vegetables into it and set aside.

Place the eggs, Tabasco Sauce, sugar, salt, and pepper in a blender and blend until the eggs are beaten. Add the milk and half and half and blend until combined. Add the flour and blend until smooth. Pour the mixture over the vegetables and place the baking dish in a pan of hot water, making sure that the water does not come more than 1/2 way up the sides of the dish. Bake in a 325 degree oven for 45 minutes or until the pudding is set.

Remove the dish from the oven and the water bath. Immediately sprinkle the cheese over the top and let sit for 3 to 4 minutes until the cheese melts. Serve at once.

Serves 4 to 6.

Corn-Chile Pudding

INDIAN FRY BREAD

Much of the food that the world now enjoys and takes for granted was unknown outside of the Americas until the fifteenth and sixteenth centuries. The American Indians cultivated pumpkins, beans, squash, melons, and corn for thousands of years before the Europeans discovered the New World.

Conversely these explorers brought new food stuffs to the Americas and introduced the Indians to beef, pork, and wheat. This fry bread is a simple way the native people used their new-found wheat flour and lard to make a bread that not only was good by itself but could be used as a simple, edible container for some of the indigenous food they had eaten for centuries.

Sopaipillas are the Mexican version of fry bread. The addition of a small amount of sugar to the batter creates a slightly sweet bread that, when served warm with honey, is the perfect accompaniment to a meal redolent of chile.

3	cups all-purpose flour
2	teaspoons baking powder
1/2	teaspoon salt
1	cup warm water
2	quarts vegetable oil for frying

Mix the flour, baking powder, and salt together, pour in the warm water and mix, then knead until the dough is soft not sticky, adding more flour or water if necessary.

Place in a bowl, cover, and let sit for 15 minutes. Divide the dough into 12 equal-sized balls. Roll each ball out until it is approximately 5 inches in diameter and 1/4-inch thick and poke a hole in the middle.

Heat the oil in a deep, heavy pan or large cast iron skillet to 375 degrees. Drop the breads, one at a time, in the hot oil and fry, turning, until golden.

Serve with butter, jam, or honey. Or use to make Indian Tacos (see recipe on page 36).

Makes 12 pieces.

Indian Fry Bread

SAUTÉED CORN AND GREEN CHILE

Although you can use frozen corn this dish is best made with the freshest sweet corn you can find. Take home ears of white or yellow corn from the farmers market, and sauté them with freshly roasted green chile, tomatoes, and bell pepper for an excellent side dish with baked ham or roast chicken.

8	ears of fresh white or yellow corn (can use frozen)
2	tablespoons olive oil
1	yellow onion, chopped
1	medium red bell pepper, seeds and membranes removed, chopped
2	ripe, red tomatoes, peeled and chopped
2	mild, long green chiles, roasted, peeled, seeded, and chopped
1/2	teaspoon salt
1/2	teaspoon freshly ground black pepper
1	teaspoon chopped fresh parsley

Using a sharp knife, cut the kernels off the corn cobs, and scrape the cob to get all the juice.

Heat the oil in a cast iron skillet and sauté the onion and bell pepper for 3 to 4 minutes or until slightly soft. Add the tomato, chile, salt, pepper, and parsley and stir. Then stir in the corn, cover, and let simmer over low heat, stirring occasionally, for 15 to 20 minutes until the corn is tender.

Serves 4 to 6.

FRUIT CHIMICHANGAS

Chimichangas are deep fried flour tortillas with meat, vegetable, or fruit filling. They are especially popular in Arizona. You can use a wide variety of fruit, including prepared pie fillings and jams, to make dessert chimichangas.

12	**flour tortillas**
2	**cups prepared cherry, pineapple, or blueberry pie filling**
	Oil for deep fat frying
	Powdered sugar

Spoon 3 tablespoons of filling down the middle of each tortilla. Fold in the ends of the tortilla, then roll the tortilla up and secure with a toothpick. The shape is similar to an egg roll.

Heat the oil to 375 degrees and drop the chimichangas one or two at a time and fry until golden. Drain on paper towels, lightly dust with powdered sugar, and serve warm with ice cream.

Serves 10 to 12.

EMPANANDAS (Fruit Turnovers)

Empanada means "that which is covered with bread." This was most possibly an easy-to-eat finger food in medieval Spain before forks were commonplace. The conquistadors no doubt brought it to the New World where it became extremely popular. Although empanadas are filled with a myriad of things—finely chopped meat, garlic, onions, fish, rice, or fruit—in the Southwest they are most often served stuffed with a fruit filling and topped with ice cream.

2	cups all-purpose flour
1	teaspoon salt
2/3	cup solid shortening
6 to 8	teaspoons cold water
6	heaping teaspoons prepared mincemeat
6	heaping teaspoons apricot preserves
2	teaspoons brandy, divided
1	egg, lightly beaten
	Powdered sugar
	Vanilla ice cream

Preheat oven to 375 degrees.

Mix the flour and salt together in a large bowl, then cut in the shortening with a pastry cutter. Stir the cold water in and mix to make a smooth dough. Place the dough on a lightly floured pastry board and roll out to 1/4-inch thick. Cut the dough into 12 equal-sized circles.

Mix 1 teaspoon of the brandy with the mincemeat and 1 teaspoon of the brandy with the apricot preserves. Place a heaping teaspoon of the mincemeat filling on 6 of the circles and a heaping teaspoon of the apricot filling on 6 of the circles. Fold each circle of dough over the filling so that it makes a semi-circle. Crimp the edges of the dough with a fork or the blunt side of a knife.

Place the empanadas on a baking sheet, brush with egg, and bake in a 375 degree oven for 15 to 20 minutes or until golden. Sprinkle with powdered sugar and serve warm with vanilla ice cream.

Makes 12 empanadas.

Empanadas (Fruit Turnovers)

MEXICAN-STYLE FLAN

Often called the national dessert of Mexico, this is one of the favorites in the Southwest.

1	cup brown sugar
2	teaspoons vanilla
3/4	cup sugar
4	eggs, lightly beaten
3	cups milk

Preheat oven to 350 degrees.

Divide the brown sugar equally among four custard cups. Put the cups in a large pan that has enough water to come halfway up the sides of the cups. Over medium heat, bring the water to a boil. When the sugar has melted and turns a golden brown color, take a pair of kitchen tongs and tilt the cups around until the caramelized sugar coats the inside of the cup about halfway up. Remove the cups from the water and let them cool. Beat the vanilla and sugar into the eggs. Then gradually beat in the milk. When the sugar has completely dissolved, pour the liquid into the custard cups. Place the cups in a baking pan with about an inch of water. Bake in a 350 degree oven for 1 hour. Turn the flan out onto small serving plates and let cool.

Serves 4.

Mexican-Style Flan

BISCOCHITOS

The debate rages on as to the name of this cookie which is a variation of the Indian sugar cookie. These cookies are called biscochos or puchitas in some areas of the Southwest.

Biscochitos are the official cookie of the state of New Mexico and are traditionally served during the holidays.

Over the years many people have asked me to develop a recipe to make biscochitos using something other than lard. I have tried butter, margarine, and vegetable shortening but none of these has been successful so I continue to make them with lard and cut down on my fat and calories another day in other ways.

1-1/2	cups lard
1	cup sugar
1	egg
1/2	cup water or white wine
2	teaspoons baking powder
2	teaspoons ground anise seeds
4	cups all-purpose flour
1	teaspoon salt
1/2	cup sugar
1	tablespoon ground cinnamon

Cream the lard and the cup of sugar together until it is light and fluffy. Add the egg, water, anise seeds, flour, and salt. Mix thoroughly.

Place the dough on a lightly floured board and roll out to 1/4-inch thick and cut into diamond shapes approximately 2 inches long. Place the cookies on a cookie sheet and bake in a 350 degree oven for 10 minutes or until done.

Mix the 1/2 cup sugar with the cinnamon. Remove the cookies from the cookie sheet and gently roll them in the sugar and cinnamon mixture while they are still slightly warm.

Let cool and store in a tightly closed container.

Makes approximately 2 dozen cookies.